OTHER HELEN EXLEY GIFTBOOKS:

Brothers!	To my Daughter with Love
Wishing you the Best Birthday Ever!	Thank Heavens for Friends
	My Memories: A Grandmothers
Congratulations on your Graduation	Record Book
	To a very special Grandpa
In Praise and Celebration of Sisters	Daughters...
To a very special Mother	The Love Between Mothers
Dads...	and Sons

Dedicated to my own special brother, Deon – Helen

Published simultaneously in 1998 by Exley Publications LLC in the
USA and Exley Publications Ltd in Great Britain.

12 11 10 9 8 7 6 5 4 3 2 1

Copyright © Helen Exley 1998
ISBN 1-86187-098-1

A copy of the CIP data is available from the British Library on request.
Written by Pam Brown
Edited by Helen Exley
Illustrated by Juliette Clarke
Printed and bound in Hungary

Exley Publications Ltd, 16 Chalk Hill, Watford, Herts WD1 4BN, UK.
Exley Publications LLC, 232 Madison Avenue, Suite 1206,
NY 10016, USA.

'TO A VERY SPECIAL'® AND 'TO-GIVE-AND-TO-KEEP'® ARE
REGISTERED TRADE MARKS OF EXLEY PUBLICATIONS LTD AND
EXLEY PUBLICATIONS LLC.

To a very special
BROTHER

Written by Pam Brown
Illustrated by Juliette Clarke

We share so much – the memories of
our upbringing, our parents, our
early days. You will always be close,
a very special part of my life.

A HELEN EXLEY GIFTBOOK

EXLEY
NEW YORK • WATFORD, UK

THANK YOU FOR EVERYTHING

Thank you for always being there for me – however many the miles between us. Your voice on the phone, remembering my birthday, your writing on an envelope, an e-mail with vital news, your special knock, your grin, the sure clasp of your hand – mean it is all going to come right.

...

A good brother looks at a rotten fence post,

a gap in the floor boards, a leaking pipe – and sighs

and says "I'll have a go...."

And does.

Thank you for rescuing me so often.

And all for the price of a cup of tea.

...

Thank you for persuading me when I left home that

the garage was far enough for one evening.

Thank you for bringing me out a Coke

and a sandwich.

Thank you for getting me back in before our

parents noticed that I'd gone.

...

Thank you for being there when I've needed you.

For mending things and unravelling things and

backing me up when I felt all alone.

How do people manage without a brother?

...

TOTAL SUPPORT

A brother somehow makes you feel secure.
Anchored into life. Certain that whatever happens
someone will be there to help you up, dust you
down and set you on your way. A contemporary
who understands your hopes and your fears.
Always.

...

The noisiest of brothers can miraculously become
the quietest when you are poorly.

...

Wherever you go, whatever you do, somehow your
brother is there.

...

A loving brother is the best comfort in distress.

...

Brothers and sisters see each others' beginnings.
Know the struggles and mistakes, the excitement.
They shout each other on.
And cheer the victories.
And give each other courage in the darker days.

...

Brothers warn, scold, growl, complain – but are
always there when you really need them.

...

A good brother is the anchor that never breaks or
shifts in any storm. Holds fast forever.

...

KIND AND STRONG

A kind brother can see you through a lifetime.

…

Some brothers can mend fuses and clear drains and paint ceilings and take cuttings and find out why the car won't go. Some brothers have other gifts. You've always been there when I needed you. You help to hold my life together. ·

With a tack or two, a length of sellotape, a bit of string, a dab of glue.

And a kind arm round my shoulders.

…

Enormous elder brothers can be very understanding when it comes to the funeral of a pet mouse.

…

Everything brothers do has affection in it. And so – is extra special.

…

Brothers scold and criticize, but when they praise you – you know you've done wonders. Brothers get cross if you sniffle but know when you are really ill or really unhappy – and help sort things out. Brothers are there when you need them. Kind and funny and strong.

...

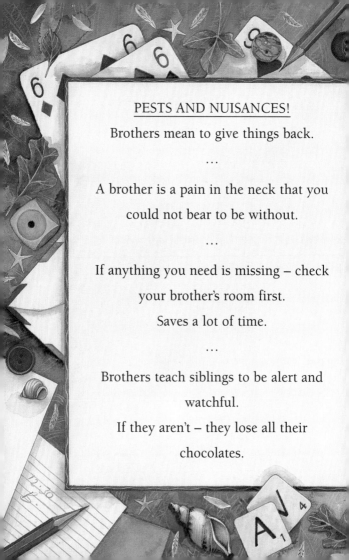

PESTS AND NUISANCES!

Brothers mean to give things back.

…

A brother is a pain in the neck that you
could not bear to be without.

…

If anything you need is missing – check
your brother's room first.
Saves a lot of time.

…

Brothers teach siblings to be alert and
watchful.
If they aren't – they lose all their
chocolates.

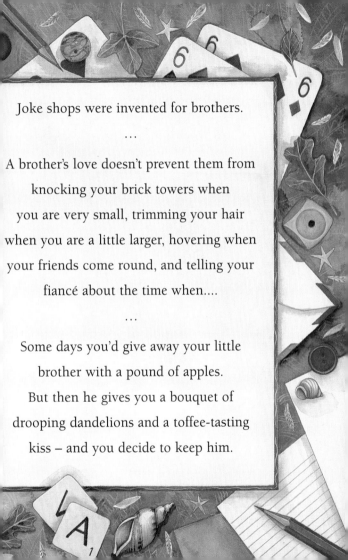

Joke shops were invented for brothers.

...

A brother's love doesn't prevent them from
knocking your brick towers when
you are very small, trimming your hair
when you are a little larger, hovering when
your friends come round, and telling your
fiancé about the time when....

...

Some days you'd give away your little
brother with a pound of apples.
But then he gives you a bouquet of
drooping dandelions and a toffee-tasting
kiss – and you decide to keep him.

NO ONE KNOWS ME SO WELL

Such a big world and everything to learn.

So many strangers. So many choices.

How good to know you're there – my first

companion and first friend.

With you I can relax and smile, knowing you

understand, and accept me as I am.

...

No one is quite like a brother for
no one knows so much about you.
No one understands the reasons
for everything you do as he does.

…

We have seen each other
as no one else has ever done.
Scared out of our wits by owls and shadows.
Muddied and bloodied by secret fights.
Weeping for hidden sorrows.
And so bound close forever.

…

There isn't any other relationship quite like that of
siblings – the memories and the affection run deep
beneath all other loves.

…

However difficult the road ahead
we'll travel it together.

…

THEY SEE RIGHT THROUGH YOU!

Conceit doesn't last long in a family.

They read the press notices

– and fall about laughing.

…

A brother is never put out by changes in your

status or appearance.

He knows very well that underneath you are the

child he had to retrieve from the garage roof.

…

Here we are, grown.

Respected people. Fairly dignified.

Reliable. A little dull

– but true and tried.

No one suspects that we

relish our memories

of mud and scummy ponds

and clambering in trees.

…

CIVIL WAR!

No one can needle you like a brother.

He's been practising for years.

…

Brothers know exactly how to make you squeal like
a pig in the middle of a silent solemnity.
And how to look absolutely astonished...
and appalled.

…

A brother never forgets the time you shoved him in
the muck pile.
Even after forty years.

...

You always know when you're talking too much.
Your brother is standing directly behind your
companion – making duck faces.

...

A day when a brother falls for a plastic biscuit, a
rubber fried egg or a puddle of imitation ink on
their homework is never a day wasted.

...

Small brothers have a way of saying something
loving or funny or sad
– the very moment you'd decided to
drop them over the local bridge.
That's how small brothers survive.

...

IDIOTS, OAFS AND SILLY-BILLIES

Brothers, from babyhood onwards, have
an affinity with mud.

…

Turn your back on a brother for a second,
and he's gone.

Locked in the loo.

Half-way up a ladder.

Stuck in a tree.

…

Brothers knees heal slowly – because they keep
lifting up the band-aid to check.

We can put men on the moon – but no one as yet
has found a way to keep up a little brother's socks.

…

Brothers stand on your bed to reach a shelf –
in muddy boots.

…

Brothers remember one's birthday – usually about
three weeks late.

…

Brothers are often wonderfully gifted in making up
excuses – the trouble is, they can get carried away.
Few teachers will accept the fact that a jaguar
barred the way to school – or that a
flash flood carried off missing homework.

…

The games brothers organise are louder, dirtier and
far more dangerous than other games.
More fun.

…

MEMORIES

A brother holds a thousand memories
of our shared past – mud-smeared, grass-stained,
jammy-mouthed – drumming our heels in fury,
locked in soundless grief, laughing until we toppled
from our chairs!

…

I treasure them all – the plots, the secrets, the
surprises. The times you rescued me.
The times I rescued you.
There will be greater loves – but none so deeply
rooted as that between siblings.

…

Time cannot alter us – only lend us strange
disguises.
Others will be fooled – see us as heroes or cowards,
victors or vanquished, achievers or failures.
But we see one another as we are – as we have
always been.
You are the brother of my childhood
– as kind, as constant
– as mischievous, as loving.

…

To the world we may be capable, efficient – even
sophisticated.
But you and I remember mud and bonfires, the
solemn burial of mice, dressing up and sword
fights. Shared secrets. Shared terrors. Shared
laughter.
I raise my glass to you....
The real you. The real me.

…

I'LL TELL MY BROTHER ON YOU!

How could I have got through childhood
without you there to see off bullies,
clean off mud, find my missing shoes,
unravel equations, lend me your protractor?

…

Brothers seem to regard their brothers or sisters as a
necessary evil – till they are in trouble.
When they roar to the rescue, red-eyed and
breathing fire.

…

Brothers are the people you turn to when no one
else will do.

…

How very good it is to know that one has a brother
who will Sort Things Out.

…

Brothers and sisters spend most of their early life
getting each other in and out of trouble.
This can extend into adulthood, and, given half a
chance, to extreme old age.

…

"I'll tell my brother on you."
The cry goes back to the cave.
The ultimate deterrent.
Thank you for all the times you rescued me.
Or got thumped, trying.

…

ROOTS, BONDS

A brother's life is a part of one's own life –
your roots so intertwined that each affects
each other all your days.

…

How good it is to know
– when I have to be dignified
and sensible and smart,
that someone in the company
will look across and smile
– knowing exactly who I am
knowing how I feel.
My touchstone. My reminder.
My unbreakable link with reality.

…

New friends, new loves, must guess what made you what you are. But we have shared fears and sorrows, triumphs and excitements and all those sillinesses that families treasure and that no one else can ever understand.

We've made a splendid team!

...

Your life and mine are joined together at the root. Whatever we've become, however different the paths we've taken, the memories of those secrets, those adventures, sorrows, pleasures – will be with us forever and forever.

Dear brother, dear friend....

...

ALL LIFE LONG

Friends go. Lovers go.

But brothers stay around.

They sometimes say

"I told you so"

or call you a silly idiot.

Or just think it and say nuthin'.

But the friendship's there.

The loyalty.

The love....

...

All my life I've known that,

however much you growl at times,

however much you tease,

however much you criticize,

you're still my brother and my

friend. We've shared so much,

good and bad. We need each other.

And I hope we always will.

...

All life long our thoughts and ways interweave –
and bind us ever closer. For whatever distance
separates us, whatever circumstance divides us –
we are family.

…

A brother's love is not confused by sentiment and
dreams – it is an enduring thing – steady and
unchanged by circumstances.
It lasts life long.
A brother knows us as we are.
Accepts us as we are
And goes on loving, knowing all our faults and
frailties.

…

No one can be utterly alone with a brother – a
brother like you.
However far away you are I sense your life, your
smile, your kindness, your concern.

…